VARIATION 1

Easier:

ANDREW LLOYD WEBBER

VARIATIONS 1-4

FOR CELLO AND PIANO

HAL•LEONARD®
CORPORATION

7777 W. BLUEMOUND RD. P.O. BOX 13819 MILWAUKEE, WI 53213

VARIATIONS
1-4

Music by Andrew Lloyd Webber
Arranged for cello and piano by Laurence Roman
Cello part edited by Julian Lloyd Webber

VARIATION 2

VARIATION 4